African Magic Series

CONNECTING WITH YOUR ANCESTORS

MONIQUE JOINER SIEDLAK

Oshun
Publications

ISBN: 978-1-950378-39-5

Publisher

Oshun Publications, LLC

Want to learn about African Magic, Wicca, or even Reiki while cleaning your home, exercising, or driving to work? I know it's tough these days to simply find the time to relax and curl up with a good book. This is why I'm delighted to share that I have books available in audiobook format.

Best of all, you can get the audiobook version of this book or any other book by me for free as part of a 30-day Audible trial.

Members get free audiobooks every month and exclusive discounts. It's an excellent way to explore and determine if audiobook learning works for you.

If you're not satisfied, you can cancel anytime within the trial period. You won't be charged, and you can still keep your book. To choose your free audiobook, visit:

www.mojosiedlak.com/free-audiobooks

Books in Series

African Spirituality Beliefs and Practices
Hoodoo
Seven African Powers: The Orishas
Cooking for the Orishas
Lucumi: The Ways of Santeria
Voodoo of Louisiana
Haitian Vodou
Orishas of Trinidad

Contents

Introduction

Throughout history, various forms of ancestral communication and worship have been vital, integral parts of many great cultures and religions. Wherever you may be from, chances are your ancestors practiced some form of ancestral communication. From the Gaelic Celts who celebrate Samhain to the Mexican Día de Muertos, forms of ancestor worship have massively influenced modern culture.

Ancestral communication can be traced back to mankind's earliest people because as long as there has been the concept of an afterlife, we have prayed to those sent there. Nearly every great culture had some form of ancestral communication. The ancient Greeks would create small shrines in their homes to honor the dead. Ancient Chinese emperors would hold massive festivals to worship their ancestors. Also, every pre-Columbian civilization in the Americas practiced worshiping and presenting offerings to their dead.

Of course, you may ask, "But all of those cultures are long gone; why do we not practice ancestral communication anymore?" Well, you will be happy to know many modern cultures do still practice ancestral communication in one form or another. Anyone familiar with Catholicism, Anglicanism, or

Eastern Orthodoxy may know of All Saints' Day and All Souls' Day. Which, in the western church, are observed every November 1st and 2nd, respectively, right after Halloween. In Korea, they practice a few ceremonies called Jesa; typically, these ceremonies are performed on the anniversary of an ancestor's death. In addition to services performed on a specific anniversary, there are also ancestral rites held on the 10th lunar month and tea ceremonies held four times a year on significant anniversaries. It is safe to say that Korean ancestors get a lot of love.

Aside from established religion, most of us have performed some kind of ancestral worship before. It may have been visiting the grave of a deceased family member and placing some flowers for them or having a row of pictures on your mantelpiece. Regardless of how you decide to honor your ancestors, they are there, and they appreciate it. Even if you don't have graves to visit or pictures to place, there are endless of other ways in which you can celebrate and honor your ancestors. As this book continues, we will examine them one by one.

ONE

Who Are Our Ancestors?

O ur ancestors are those who came before, not just your great-grandparents but also their great-grandparents and so on. It's your entire bloodline from the first of your family name up to your recent relatives. Our ancestors are who we have to thank for us being here; without them fighting for survival over the centuries, we would never have existed. For that, I think the ancestors of every person deserve some well-earned respect and admiration.

WHO IS AN ANCESTOR?

To the uninitiated, it may seem a bit confusing seeing all this talk of ancestors but not understanding what kind of being they are. To put it simply, they are spirits, the souls of the dead. But do not fear, we won't be practicing black magic or raising the dead; we simply want to talk with them. We want to learn from them, share their knowledge, and give them some company in the afterlife.

Some religions claim that the spirits of the dead are unreachable on the other side, but the practice has shown otherwise. By the conclusion of this book, you will have the tools available for you to contact your forebears and seek their wisdom in life.

WHO ARE YOUR ANCESTORS?

Now, how do we figure out who your ancestors are? Your close relatives should be easy to find out about. Asking a parent, grandparent, or maybe some elder relative about your family can shed a lot of light on your familial past.

But, of course, your recent ancestors are not the only ones we will be communicating with. We may need to delve deeper into your heritage to get a clearer idea of your ancestors.

Were they fearsome warriors of a warlike nation? Maybe they were peaceful subsistence farmers. You may have some great leaders, inventors, or philosophers in your ancestry. Of course, it is hard to find specifics, but a bit of research can go a long way.

Finding the origin of your parents' family names and searching for any well-known people who may share that name or a variety of it can be a great place to start.

There are always DNA kits and ancestry tests that you can pay for too, but I do not think they are necessary. Your ancestors will reveal themselves to you over time, and as you spend more time with them, they will share more with you.

DISCOVERING Our Ancestors

We have covered who your ancestors are and what kind of being they are, but we have yet to touch on where they are. Every single belief system has a different name for it, whether it be Heaven, the Summerland, Valhalla, or another. Regardless of the name, it is more or less the same place.

The Astral Plane is where we will find our ancestors. This is a plane of existence separated from our world yet intertwined with its very fabric. This is the realm of spirits. How it looks and is structured, we can only guess. Some people claim to be able to see it or even visit it. Still, for every person, I believe, the experience is different.

As well as inhabiting the Astral Plane, our ancestors are a part of us. We have a blood bond connecting us to them. A portion of them lives in us, which makes forming a connection to them very easy. As we go forward through this book, we will explore ways of making that connection and contacting their plane of existence.

I genuinely hold the belief that everyone should discover their ancestors. In modern society, people far too often forget their origins, where they came from, and who they have to thank. By finding our ancestors and making contact with them, we can rediscover a part of who we are that has been long forgotten.

TWO

Why Communicate With Your Ancestors?

N ow that we have learned so much about our ancestors, you may start to wonder why we are trying to contact them. There is this notion of "out of sight, out of mind" regarding the dead in this day and age. But it is a crucial part of every person's spiritual journey to form this connection with their forebears. The ancestors are there to assist us in life, and by ignoring them, we are missing out on an incredible hoard of wisdom and knowledge. Our spiritual growth benefits massively from making bonds with the world around us. Our ancestors are part of our world just as much as the birds outside the window.

COMMUNICATING With Your Ancestors

As we explore talking with the ancestors in this book, you will be presented with various techniques for contacting them. Still, before we get to any of that, we should talk about the benefits and how we can grow by spending time with them. Creating a bond with the ancestors is more than just keeping them company or asking for their help; it is a form of spiritual enlightenment.

. . .

REASONS FOR COMMUNICATING

Each one of us has the sacrifices of our ancestors to thank for our life. They built the foundations of our existence and, therefore, are deserving of our eternal gratitude and reverence. An essential way of showing our gratitude is through the actions we perform in our daily life. The ancestors did not sacrifice so much for you to be a harmful and selfish person. Being a loving and kind person is the first step toward thanking our ancestors and growing as a person.

In our lives, we face many challenges that are, in fact, a result of our ancestral heritage. Many of us may suffer from an addictive personality, mental illness, a predisposition toward violence, and a myriad of other conditions passed down to us from those who came before. It may seem unfair that we should be shouldered with the burdens of our ancestors, but just as we can heal by making the right choices for ourselves, we can help our ancestors heal. Many people think that it is our duty to help our ancestors overcome their flaws in death so they may live a peaceful afterlife. In assisting them to overcome their weaknesses, we also help ourselves grow as people. So we address the issues we have been given.

For example, if you have a family history of depression, then be vigilant for the signs of it in yourself and seek help, if any, appear. Similarly, for health conditions, if you have a history of certain diseases in your family, it would be wise to have frequent check-ups. Your ancestors want you to avoid the mistakes they made. They are here to guide you on your journey toward a fulfilled potential. And in achieving your potential, you bring honor and the greatest form of gratitude to your ancestors.

As well as remedying potential issues passed down to us, we can help our ancestors and ourselves balance our karma. Whether you believe in karma or not, it is an integral part of our bond with our ancestors. Not all of our ancestors were ethical people in their physical lives. We may have some awful people in our lineage, but we can help them atone and, in turn, take a better direction in our own lives. How? Through good acts, of course! Performing acts of charity and kindness and living an ethical life dedicated to the ancestors will help bring balance to your bloodline. It will help your ancestors atone for their wrongdoings and will allow you to take a more fulfilling path in life with their support.

When we decide to help our ancestors on their journey to spiritual balance, they may choose to assist us in return. Through dreams, they may send us signs and messages. Through meditation, they may speak words of wisdom to us. They may even positively influence things in our favor in life to help us on our path forward. We stand to gain so much from having a positive relationship with our ancestors.

THREE

Spiritually Connecting With Your Ancestors

I n this chapter, we will take our first tentative steps toward starting our first proper dialogue with the ancestors. This first contact must be made respectfully, that you introduce yourself, and that you are in the right mindset to receive feedback from your ancestors' spirits.

HOW TO SPIRITUALLY Connect With Your Ancestors

Making your first actual communication with the ancestors is an exciting experience, but do not be lured into the trap of doing too much too fast. Just as with meeting people in real life, you should start small. A simple greeting and introduction are the ideal way to make the first contact with your ancestors. Of course, they already know who you are—they are a part of you after all—but manners are essential.

Let us set the scene. For your first communication, you want to be somewhere comfortable and quiet. This is an intimate experience, and you do not want interruptions if you can avoid it. Use some sage or incense to cleanse the air around you. A small bowl of water on the ground to wash your hands is a powerful action of cleansing too. Finally, seat yourself in a comfortable position. You can assume a meditative pose or take a seat in a chair; whatever you prefer most is best.

Now comes time for the prayer. If you have a background in Christianity, you've probably started with a prayer with "Please God" or "Holy Father" at some time in your life. Think of these prayers to the ancestors in a similar light. Talk with respect and reverence such as "Great Ancestors" or "I welcome you, Ancestors." Make sure your breathing is slow and calm, and try to clear your mind of everything except what you wish to say. Then simply introduce yourself as you would to an acquaintance, and let your ancestors know a bit about yourself.

For this first communication, we will not do much more than this. This is our initial correspondence. You can perform this prayer for a few days if you wish, adding different details each time, sharing stories, and telling them about your goals in life.

Remember always to close off your prayer with a goodbye. It may seem like something unimportant and easy to forget. Still, whenever you open a connection to the ancestors, you must remember to close it. In the same way, you may open a fridge to retrieve a refreshing drink of water and then close it again so as not to waste electricity. You should treat this connection the same. The energy of the ancestors is precious and should not be wasted. So end every prayer with a "thank you" and a "goodbye."

THE IMPORTANCE of Respect

As mentioned above, respect is essential. The ancestors are age-old spirits, and many generations may separate them from you. Still, one thing that transcends any boundaries of time or age is respect. If we compose ourselves calmly and respectfully, show manners and kindness, and act with generosity toward our ancestors, we will get the same treatment in return. On the other hand, if we are disrespectful and demanding toward our ancestors, they will not be inclined to help us or share their knowledge. We must act in a manner that shows us as worthy of their energy and wisdom.

FOUR

Creating a Shrine

The next big step in our ancestral communication has a shrine or altar at which we can say prayers, perform rituals, and present gifts. A shrine will be your hub of spiritual activity and, therefore, should be made with care and love. This will be the gateway between realms that allows your ancestors to meet you.

HOW TO BUILD Your Shrine

Building a shrine is crucial to our efforts at communicating, and although it may seem a lot of work at first glance, it is undoubtedly worth it in the long run. This holy place will heighten our connection with our ancestors. Aside from the actual benefits of having a finished shrine, the actual process of building it is a healing one. Devoting your time and effort into something so pure and spiritual is good for the soul, and the happier you are with your shrine, the happier your ancestors will be.

Starting with the basics, we will go step by step through the process of building a shrine for our ancestors.

- First, we want to find a nice space for your shrine. Start your shrine building in a pleasant, quiet area, preferably some-where where it will not be disturbed by curious hands. Depending on your preference, you can have it in a well-lit area with a view to the outside or a dim room. It doesn't make a difference. Whatever speaks to you while creating your place of prayer will work fine.

I would recommend not building your shrine in a bedroom if you can avoid it. Your shrine will be a center of spiritual activity, and the energy around it may make it hard for sensitive people to sleep and relax in the same room as it.

- Second, once we have chosen an area, we must cleanse it. Make sure the space is uncluttered and cleaned of any dust. Burn some sage or incense of your choice in the area to cleanse the air. With a clean cloth and some plain water, wipe down the surfaces around your shrine. Anywhere you may be sitting during prayer or wherever you plan to put items for rituals.

- Third, we need to lay down a piece of cloth over the altar of our shrine, the centerpiece, if you will. A plain white cloth will be fine because it is a great neutral color, but choose whatever color speaks to you. The cloth symbolizes a separa-tion of our world and the realm between them and us. Every-thing below the cloth belongs to our world, and everything on top of the cloth is shared with them.

- Fourth, we need items of ancestral value to place on our shrine, whether this is a picture of a deceased relative, a family heirloom, or a relic of your heritage. Be careful, putting too many things on your shrine, though. We do not want it too cluttered. It is far better to focus your energy on a small number of items than have it spread across too many.

Also, be careful placing a picture with people other than the specific ancestor you wish to contact on the shrine. You do not want to attract other spirits besides your ancestors. If the other person in the picture is still alive, we should not involve them in our ancestral affairs.

- Fifth and last, place a candle and a bowl of clean water on the altar or centerpiece of your shrine. When we make contact with our ancestors in any way, we will light the candle to call on them.

Now that you have built your shrine, you will need to activate it and make your first contact through it. Make sure you are prepared, your mind is clear, and your body is relaxed. You will have already spoken to your ancestors at this point. Still, communication through a shrine is much more intense if done correctly.

Now step by step, I will guide you through the process of activating your shrine.

- First, we must light our candle. This signals to the spirits that you are there and that they are welcome to join you.

- Second, take a few deep breaths, calm yourself, and clear your mind. Invite your ancestors to speak with you at the shrine. Calling on them out loud is best, but if you must do it quietly, that will work too. Just make sure that regardless, you speak from the heart. If you cannot decide on the way to call upon them, keeping it simple is always fine. Something along the lines of "Ancestors, I ask you to join me here at my shrine, please come and speak with me" will work perfectly.

- Third, after repeating your call to the spirits as many times as you feel you need to, take a minute of silence to center yourself once more. I would suggest, before going any further, that you set boundaries with the spirits that have joined you. Lay down the spaces of your home where they may interact with you and the off-limits areas. We do not want our dreams disturbed by talkative spirits, nor do we want our personal space and privacy invaded.

- Fourth, open yourself to questions, requests, and negotiations. Your ancestors may ask for gifts or offerings, or they may ask questions about you and about people you may both know. Feel free to answer them as long as you are comfortable.

You are here to form a bond with them after all, and learning about each other is the best way to do that.

Keep in mind you should always be prepared to say no. They might have a question you are not able to or comfortable answering or a request you cannot fulfill. Never be scared to say no. You are the one who opened the dialogue, and you can close it. Treat them as if they were a normal human being in the room with you. Have the same boundaries that you would with any other person.

• Fifth and last, remember to close the connection when you are finished. After your conversation with the spirits, say thank you and goodbye, and close the dialogue between you and them. Put out the candle and cleanse the room once more with incense.

THE RIGHT TIME

The time you choose to talk with your ancestors may affect the intensity of the experience. Many cultures recognize moon cycles as important times of spiritual activity. The new moon is a particularly powerful spiritual phase that you can use to bolster your prayers and ceremonies. Aside from moon cycles, some particular days and months offer heightened activity.

• Samhain/All Souls' Day/Día de Muertos or other significant days honoring the dead in your family's religious or cultural background.

• Deathdays or birthdays of specific ancestors you are trying to reach out to.

• Even your birthday is a powerful time of the year. You can reach out to ancestors who have had their days of birth and death forgotten on this day.

• The month of October. This time of the calendar year has been observed for centuries to have massively heightened spiritual activity. Many consider this is the time of year when the spiritual realm and this world are at their closest.

. . .

OFFERINGS for the Ancestors

You may feel slightly lost picking out offerings for the honored dead. Still, fear not, there are plenty of offerings that nearly all dead appreciate. If you have a particular ancestor in mind for your offerings and you have an idea of what they liked, then, of course, you should offer something specific. If your deceased grandfather liked smoking his pipe, a bowl of tobacco would be appreciated. If your deceased aunt had a fondness for sweets and treats, a handful of candy would go down well. If you have a recipe book passed down on one side of the family, try and recreate one of the dishes. As for generalized offerings that all dead may enjoy, you can try some of the following:

- A bowl of clean water. We have already established this as a part of every prayer ceremony
- Wine or alcohol
- Flowers, herbs, and incense
- Coins, simple jewelry, or gemstones
- Hot aromatic tea or coffee
- Tobacco
- Candy, desserts, and sugary food or drink
- Freshly peeled and cut fruits
- A hearty home-cooked meal

Not many senses cross into the spiritual realm, but it seems our ancestors have kept their sense of smell. They have a particular fondness for aromatic and sweet-smelling foods, flowers, and incense. Anything with a pleasant smell may go down well as an offering to them. A convenient way of including your ancestors in family gatherings over holiday periods is by putting aside a small portion of whatever you prepared for your living family. Simply present it to the ancestors before it cools or reheating it later before offering.

FIVE

Working With Our Ancestors

I n this final chapter, you will be presented with all the tools to build a healthy, beneficial, and long-lasting relationship with your ancestors. Taking what we have already learned in terms of prayer and offerings, we will build upon this knowledge by learning about dream work. This will include rituals and some more advanced prayer techniques.

WHAT IS DREAMWORK?

Dreamwork is the practice of inviting your ancestors into your dreams to provide you with visions and guidance on current issues in your life or, potentially, problems that are yet to come. It may seem a scary concept to let spirits into your dreams, but you are in full control. You invite them in, and if at any point you feel uncomfortable, you need only wake up.

A GUIDE to Dream Work

Being blessed with a dream is a rather simple process; just ask. If you have a good relationship with your ancestors, they will be eager to help. Requesting a dream from them during a ritual or prayer can be a great help in life. Keep in mind the boundaries that you previously set in your home. If your bedroom is off-limits to the ancestors, then consider sleeping in a different room that they have access to. Otherwise, you may not get as much help as you would wish. Asking about a specific issue or topic will also help the ancestors focus their energy on one point. You have centuries of wisdom at your fingertips, so feel free to ask for their assistance, and I am sure they will be happy to oblige.

HOW TO READ Your Dreams

Reading dreams can be tricky. So much is up to interpretation, but there are a few handy tricks that can help bring clarity to your blessed dreams.

- Record your dreams. Immediately after having a profound dream, note down everything you can. Prioritize highlights, the things that stand out, first, and then fill in the smaller details later. We mustn't waste the wisdom of the ancestors by forgetting what they have shown us in our dreams. So make sure you have a pen and paper near every time you go to sleep.

- Do not make any assumptions. Try not to read into your dreams too much right after having them; consult your notes over the course of the coming day and slowly pick apart the details you noted down. Try to leave logic at the door when writing down and studying your dreams. There is no logic in a dream, and, therefore, looking at them through a logical eye will just muddy the waters.

- Be completely honest with yourself. We all have dreams where we do things we may not be proud of. Sometimes illegal and immoral actions in dreams are a way of bringing attention to something your ancestors feel you need to focus on. For example, if you were to have an inappropriate sexual relationship with someone in a dream, that does not necessarily mean you desire them. It could mean your ancestors wish for you to become closer to them or even learn from them and be more like them.

• Make a note of the emotions you felt within the dream, directly after the dream, and while writing about the dream. These feelings could be a big hint toward the true meaning of the dream. For example, you may be feeling sad and melancholic while writing about a dream you had. Still, during the dream itself, you felt joy and happiness. This may be the ancestors telling you that you can handle certain situations in a better way or with a better outlook.

• Follow your gut instinct. It may be very easy to overanalyze and overthink the messages that are sent to you. Still, you must keep things simple—if you have a gut intuition about a specific situation in your dream, run with it. The chances are that feeling is correct.

THE IMPORTANCE of Rituals

Rituals are your most potent form of worshiping your ancestors. As much as they appreciate prayers and offerings, performing a full ritual of dancing, chants, candles, and offerings is a fantastic way of honoring them and ensuring a good relationship.

ANCESTOR RITUALS Around the World

Even in the modern-day, cultures from all over the world perform rituals to honor their dead. In Korea, as mentioned at the start of this book, there are frequent ceremonies and rituals held for the dead. Three particularly important Korean services are Bulcho, the Sebae bow, and Charye. Bulcho consists of clearing the weeds and rocks off of the graves of family members. The Sebae bow is a formal and ceremonial form of bowing that is often performed on noteworthy occasions and the graves of ancestors. Charye is an offering of food, liquor, and tea given to the ancestors of a family.

In Mexico, the Día de Muertos is a world-famous two-day holiday. Members of Mexican households will create shrines to their deceased family members. Many of these shrines include colorful and aromatic flowers, photos of the deceased, food and drinks, and prayers. As well as creating beautiful shrines, during Día de Muertos, there are massive and widespread celebrations. Entire towns come together to celebrate the lives of the dead through parties, parades, and public dancing.

In most West and Sub-Saharan African countries, ceremonies to honor the dead are incredibly common. They are often practiced alongside adopted religions like Christianity and Islam. Funerals are often occasions filled with much dancing and song to help the soul of the dead find their way to the ancestors. Local and tribal shamans still hold much respect, and it is not uncommon for people to visit them to perform a small ceremony to receive wisdom from the ancestors.

HOW TO PERFORM Your Own Ritual

Performing your own ritual is a case of how much work you are willing to do and the environment you have available to hold one in. The greater your ritual, the more favor you will garner, but do not aim too high, and work within your means. It would be wise to perform some research on your ancestors' religion or culture. If they followed a particular belief system, there may be some things from that which you could include in your ritual. Let's say you had North European ancestors. You could incorporate runes and traditional Germanic music into your ceremony. If your ancestors are of African stock, look into the traditional music of their people. Drum patterns can be easily imitated and will be sure to please your ancestors.

Dance is another essential part of a successful ritual. The movement and flow of a body to music or chanting is a raw form of energy and is sure to empower the spirits of your ancestors. Either develop a dance of your own or find one for yourself via your research.

Start a ritual as you would any typical communication session, and then call on your ancestors to join you in the celebration of their lives. A mixture of music and dance and a myriad of offerings will please them greatly. Always try to have your shrine as the centerpiece of your ritual. That is your spiritual hub, after all. A ritual like this once or twice a year on vital days is sure to keep you in good stead.

SAYING a Prayer to the Ancestors

Earlier, we went over briefly how to pray to the ancestors, and here, we will elaborate more on how to use this handy form of communication to enrich your days. Praying is incredibly useful for someone who may not always be at home near their shrine. A prayer can find its way to the ancestors regardless of where you are. It can be said quickly on a commute, during lunch, or while out during the day. You can personalize your prayers as well or opt for more traditional varieties. Either way, as long as you say it with heart, the meaning will get across.

HOW TO PRAY to Your Ancestors

With every prayer you say, you send a bolt of energy with a message attached to the ancestors. Therefore, every prayer grants them some small strength. Prayer is rather simple when it comes down to it; you simply need to close your eyes and focus on forming a connection. Imagine yourself writing down the words you wish to say; imagine attaching that note to a carrier pigeon and setting that bird free to fly to the heavens. The stronger your focus and the purer the sentiment in your words, the more power the prayer will have.

Conclusion

We have learned so much about our ancestors in this book. We have explored the history of our beliefs, discovered our heritage, and connected with our ancestors and built shrines for them. We have even learned how to interpret their messages to us. Now you, the reader, have all the tools you need to start your journey to true spiritual enlightenment through the wisdom of your forebears.

I call on you to prepare a ritual for your ancestors. Celebrate your new-found relationship with them and find joy in having them in your life. Appreciate them and cherish this great blessing you now have. Take their experience and apply it to your life; you will truly be able to achieve great things.

But do not stop there. Continue building upon your knowledge, expanding your horizons, and incorporating new things into your rituals. If you can, spread the word of your enlightenment. Let us bring back a reverence of our ancestors into modern society. A world with their wisdom is a world far less likely to repeat their mistakes.

References

Ancestor worship. (n.d.). Retrieved from https://www.britannica.com/topic/ancestor-worship

Antoine, D. (2020, April 10). How to Work With Your Ancestors As A Spiritual Practice. Retrieved from https://www.annasayce.com/how-to-work-with-your-ancestors-as-a-spiritual-practice/

Coppock, K. (2019, October 27). A Guide to Dead and Ancestral Worship, Altars, Offerings, and Ritual. Retrieved from https://sphereandsundry.com/a-guide-to-dead-and-ancestral-worship-altars-offerings-and-ritual/

Dragonsong, E. (n.d.). Dream Work Method: How To Understand Your Dreams*Wicca. Retrieved from https://www.wicca-spirituality.com/dream_work.html

Foor, D. (n.d.). Five Ways to Honor Your Ancestors. Retrieved from https://ancestralmedicine.org/five-ways-to-honor-your-ancestors/

Foster, S. (2011, June 14). Modern Ancestor Worship Musings. Retrieved from https://www.patheos.com/blogs/pantheon/2011/06/modern-ancestor-worship-musings/

Joyous, C. (n.d.). Learn How to Connect With Your

Ancestors With This Powerful Ritual! Retrieved from
https://apinkmoongoddess.com/learn-how-to-connect-with-
your-ancestors-with-this-powerful-ritual/

Meji, O. (2019, July 10). THE IMPORTANCE OF
HONORING THE ANCESTORS. Retrieved from
https://www.embracingspirituality.com/2014/08/18/the-
importance-of-honoring-the-ancestors/

About the Author

Monique Joiner Siedlak is a writer, witch, and warrior on a mission to awaken people to their greatest potential through the power of storytelling infused with mysticism, modern paganism, and new age spirituality. At the young age of 12, she began rigorously studying the fascinating philosophy of Wicca. By the time she was 20, she was self-initiated into the craft, and hasn't looked back ever since. To this day, she has authored over 40 books pertaining to the magick and mysteries of life.

To find out more about Monique Joiner Siedlak artistically, spiritually, and personally, feel free to visit her **official website**.

www.mojosiedlak.com

facebook.com/mojosiedlak

twitter.com/mojosiedlak

instagram.com/mojosiedlak

pinterest.com/mojosiedlak

bookbub.com/authors/monique-joiner-siedlak

More Books by Monique

Practical Magick
Wiccan Basics
Candle Magick
Wiccan Spells
Love Spells
Abundance Spells
Herb Magick
Moon Magick
Creating Your Own Spells
Gypsy Magic
Protection Magick
Celtic Magick

Personal Growth and Development
Creative Visualization
Astral Projection for Beginners
Meditation for Beginners
Reiki for Beginners
Manifesting With the Law of Attraction
Stress Management
Being an Empath Today

The Yoga Collective
Yoga for Beginners
Yoga for Stress
Yoga for Back Pain
Yoga for Weight Loss
Yoga for Flexibility
Yoga for Advanced Beginners
Yoga for Fitness
Yoga for Runners
Yoga for Energy
Yoga for Your Sex Life
Yoga: To Beat Depression and Anxiety
Yoga for Menstruation
Yoga to Detox Your Body
Yoga to Tone Your Body

A Natural Beautiful You
Creating Your Own Body Butter
Creating Your Own Body Scrub
Creating Your Own Body Spray

THANK YOU FOR READING MY BOOK! I REALLY APPRECIATE ALL OF YOUR FEEDBACK AND I LOVE TO HEAR WHAT YOU HAVE TO SAY. PLEASE LEAVE YOUR REVIEW AT YOUR FAVORITE RETAILER!

Made in the USA
Coppell, TX
22 December 2021